Lewis UNPLUGGED 2
SENYRU-HAIKU-TANKA
Lewis Colyar

Copyright @2021 by Lewis Colyar

All rights reserved. No part of this book may be reproduced in any form or by any electronic or mechanical means, including information storage and retrieval systems, without permission in writing from the publisher, except by reviewers, who may quote brief passages in a review.

This publication contains the opinions and ideas of its author. It is intended to provide helpful and informative material on the subjects addressed in the publication. The author and publisher specifically disclaim all responsibility for any liability, loss or risk, personal or otherwise, which is incurred as a consequence, directly or indirectly, of the use and application of any of the contents of this book.

WORKBOOK PRESS LLC
187 E Warm Springs Rd,
Suite B285, Las Vegas, NV 89119, USA

Website: https://workbookpress.com/
Hotline: 1-888-818-4856
Email: admin@workbookpress.com

Ordering Information:
Quantity sales. Special discounts are available on quantity purchases by corporations, associations, and others. For details, contact the publisher at the address above.

ISBN-13: 978-1-955459-76-1 (Paperback Version)
978-1-955459-77-8 (Digital Version)

REV. DATE: 06/09/2021

Lew-is UNPLUGGED 2
SENYRU-HAIKU-TANKA

by: Lewis Colyar

Table of Contents

Dedication.. 05

Dedication.. 06

Acknowledgement............................. 07

Poems.. 09-96

Author Gallery..................................... 97

Introduction

The series of Haiku that lies within this book is a part of a series of beautifully handwritten poems. These were written by none other than the classical Lewis Colyar, also known as The Dandelion Poet. He is a man who has dedicated a portion of his life to writing Haiku & now readers will be able to dive into the mind of the dandelion poet.

-Kenneth Lewis Moore

Dedication

In Memory of
Pearl Denise Strong
July 7, 1969- May 15, 2020

her dance was in her walk
she now rests with our ancestors
Juba dancers celebrate

Rest well my African Queen, may the ancestor shower you with gifts..

ACKNOWLEDGEMENT

My deepest appreciation to....

All those who encouraged me and helped me in prayer, project, and financial support to bring this book to completion;

My Third Generation Nephew

Ceyanie Dwayne DuBose Jr.

Cover Photo Credits

Artist James Robert Kessler

Scottdale, Pennsylvania

Photographer Ricco JL Martello

Pittsburgh, Pennsylvania

I want to thank also my friends who gave a list of my Senryu, Haiku,

and Tanka. They are the one who selected the poems they would like to appear in this book. Their names also appear with those selections.

late night he dances
in my head I watch and feel
the rhythm of his soul

Pearl D. Strong

what do these
three lines mean to any of us
5-7-5 sometimes

*missed education
of the alphabets
no one sang with me*

For: April Baumgardner

full moon
I'm being stalked
Shadow

*demons at my door
better damn well
wipe their feet*

Dedicate: Westlake Terrace
Youngstown, Ohio
Chase Swimming Pool
once surrounded by
housing projects
gentrification

Mississippi Sequence 7

Money Mississippi
one white lie of a whistle
death of a black boy

Emmett Louis Till August 28, 1955

Mississippi River
unable to speak
mouth filled with souls

Mississippi Sequence (Cont.)

Mississippi
Tallahatchie
Yalobusha
Yazoo Rivers
do Emmett's tears flow with you

grave memorials
how many will be along
the Mississippi

Mississippi Sequence (Cont.)

Tallahatchie River
in the breeze
Emmett's voice

Tallahatchie Bridge
sorry to hear you lost your life
you knew Emmett's story

For: Liz Shellenberger

seashell to my ear
listening for voices cast
into the ocean

For: Billie Holiday
April 7, 1915 - July 17, 1959

the haunted trees
of America
unbroken branches

the Black man
not American
as apple pie

For: Dr. Johnathan L. White

one white crayon
in the whole box
thinking out loud

church girl
unable to interpret her
late night languages

hour of decision
was it lost
setting the clocks back

Lucifer Morning Star
the face we attribute to him
as Satan

*the aging grey cat
redefining finicky
spends its days hiding*

summer evenings
I never understood why
my parents enjoyed
swatting at mosquitoes
and listening to crickets

thunderstorm
my late mother's voice
unplug everything

Inspired by: Kobayashi Issa

*a world of struggle
the ant carries its weight
evening sky*

fractions
when it was determined
we were 3/5 human

*the chicken has brought
so many to Jesus
4th Sunday dinners*

early spring morning
little girls place gardenias
left side of their hair

*the back of my mind
all my lost thoughts
what was I thinking*

little did we know
when playing the child's game
hang the Chinaman

a book of senryu
I hope the tree has the honor
for its sacrifice

*watching a sparrow
bathing I remind it to
wash behind its ears*

*child playing
cops and robbers
dual role*

For: Michael Rehling

promise land
I hope it isn't thing like
those forty acres

daring adventures
at the brink of death
that damn love scene

*if Alice were black
she wouldn't wonder
what land she was in*

*ants how quickly you
have arrived I just sat
my sandwich down*

the wind chaperoning
a dandelion wish
outside your window

seedless watermelon
the stork is on vacation
she's pregnant

dandelions wishes
butterflies
you

*final revisions
as if I'm not perfect
enough*

Noah's Ark

once they were free
the crows continued
with their flight to freedom

*dandelions and crows
reimagine each breath
season to season*

early spring morning
little girls place gardenias
left side of their hair
all are requesting to be
called Billie Holiday

For: Rosemary Breyton Schiff

late into the night
her fragrance lingers
I inhale

For: David Mckeown

evening at the pond
the lonely frog waiting
for his prince's kiss

bitter wind blowing
the wind chimes
still playing a tune

For: Heather Gillmore

bucket list
finally meeting myself
after all these years

*I love to dream
with my eyes wide open
kaleidoscope*

a man of many hats
never is he homeless
wherever he laid them

*term life insurance
invitation to plan our
transitory life*

harvest moon
bringing comfort to
lost shooting stars

summer
hot and sticky night
she's not in the mode

*the frog and pond
existing for each other
without a fairytale*

somewhere in this life
our exhales must surely meet
inhale together

*the collapse
of civilization
only ants' left*

fall
the crows have the answers
ask your questions

*dress rehearsal
chameleon can't make
its mind up*

autumn
garden of Eden
everything changed

*my copyright
on mistakes have expired
if you need a few*

*frogs croaking
down at the lake
night fishing*

*blue sky
cumulus form images
too many dead*

*looking into the
mirror who else can
I tell my troubles*

lost items
looking everywhere
I didn't put it

Dandelion Sequence

I don't know how good
my haiku
dandelions return

all my wishes
you and dandelions
aphrodisiac

floriography
the things dandelions
desire to tell us

subject and verb
dandelions are gone
autumn

funeral
the smell of dandelions
he would be happy

dandelions
unnoticed until
haiku

sun dandelions
children playing in sandboxes
how fast our childhood

no understanding
she tossed the dandelions
also my new hat

dandelions
why are you not flowers
such as yellow roses

spring dandelions
the first food source
for bees

*to smash a spider
is to deprive the world
of an artist*

after being beat
threatened
the poem was silent

the devil's music
the little angles we made
heavenly moon

COVID
a season to contemplate
disregard masks

*our silence goes
deep into this autumn night
full moon*

brightness of spring
the flower fix
weeds included

spring sale
snowperson clothing
withered carrot free

bad love experience
society teaches don't cry
be a man

homeless person
eulogy held at the gravesite
without a church home

*Christians
always being chased
by the Devil*

*Satan still knows
all the heavenly songs
sang as Lucifer*

unfinished sentence
I fail to complete it
she stormed out of the room

autumn
God wants us to know
we can all live together

*some days I believe
that the sun would like to rise
without description*

For: Billie Holiday

*I hope heaven
permits gardenias
there's a lady present*

in the rain
waiting for the bus
the two of us

*the best ideals
sometimes must be scraped
the flood*

*how lovely heaven
must have sounded to those
that was enslaved*

*when the whole earth
was filled with rainwater
to wash God's error*

*pharmaceutical
a medication for
everything possible*

spring training
a fly circles the room
dodging my swats

the very last fairytale
an eternal oasis
others damnation

retirement
I thought that I would
mimic my father
when my time came
sit on the porch and
spirit chew at files
cancer

*now I understand
education
alphabets*

AUTHOR'S GALLERY

Poster About the Theatric Reading Featuring the Author as the Executive Producer

Commonwealth of Pennsylvania

Department of Education

COMMONWEALTH SECONDARY SCHOOL DIPLOMA

This diploma is conferred upon LEWIS L. COLYAR

in recognition of having met the requirements for high school completion in accordance with the Act of the General Assembly Number 212, approved May 15, 1945.

Date Issued
01/31/83

Given under the seal of the Department of Education of the Commonwealth of Pennsylvania at Harrisburg.

270378
0317765
DEBE-569 (4-81)

SECRETARY OF EDUCATION

Author's Diploma in Pennsylvania in the Year 1983

Author's Chosen Image for Cover Creation